DOUG

Autobiography
of a Yorkshire Christian

Douglas and Eileen Higgins
on their Golden Wedding Anniversary, 16 August, 1994

DOUGLAS HIGGINS

Autobiography
of a Yorkshire Christian

THE BANNER OF TRUTH TRUST

THE BANNER OF TRUTH TRUST

3 Murrayfield Road, Edinburgh EH12 6EL, UK
P.O. Box 621, Carlisle, PA 17013, USA

© Douglas Higgins 2014
First published 2014
Reprinted 2015

ISBNs
Print: 978 1 84871 488 5
EPUB: 978 1 84871 489 2
Kindle: 978 1 84871 490 8

Typeset in 10/14 pt Sabon Oldstyle Figures at
The Banner of Truth Trust

Printed in the USA by
Versa Press, Inc.,
East Peoria, IL

Contents

Illustrations

Foreword

Douglas Higgins was a born teacher, but he was not born as a Christian. How he became one at the age of twenty-two is a valuable part of these pages. I am glad he has given us much of his life story in his own words for he has always spoken in a way which makes you want to listen. Although much of his professional life was spent as a teacher, and most notably as a teacher of art, he is a man of many gifts and many interests: a sculptor and potter, as well as a painter in oil and water-colour; an engineer; a gardener and a lover of nature in all its forms; a cyclist who covered much of England by that means. In his own church, and in numbers of others, he is known as an ever-cheerful encourager and a lover of the word of God. That he should take up a ministry of care for students from mainland China when in his nineties is typical of the life God has given him.

An invitation to a weekend in the home of Douglas and Eileen in 1962, when I had been asked to preach in Sheffield, was the beginning of what has been for me a prized friendship. At that time I noted a characteristic in my friend which has continued through the years. You needed to be in a pulpit to see it best, for it concerned his behaviour as a hearer. Sermons can be listened to in different ways, and there is one manner of listening which gives much help to a preacher even as he speaks. This belonged to Douglas. There cannot be many more eager listeners to preaching than he, and his appreciation is commonly written all over his face. If it was missing I would have reason to think there was something missing with my sermon.

In this respect, as in others, he has been a teacher by example as well as by word. What a privilege it is to have reached the centenary year of one's birth and not to have outlived one's usefulness! We thank God for a life which has been of blessing to so many.

IAIN H. MURRAY
Edinburgh
May, 2014

Preface

My desire in the publication of these pages is to bear witness to God's sovereign pleasure, power, and mercy in revealing himself in Christ Jesus, as the only Saviour of guilty, lost mankind. This truth is confirmed to all who come to him in repentance and faith. By the truth of Scripture we are thus led into true happiness here and glory to come. I hope my life will point others to depend on the same Saviour.

A number have helped me to prepare this autobiography for publication. Thanks are due especially to my daughter, Dorothy; to my son, Andrew; and to Iain Murray for his practical help. I have valued the encouragement of Professor Derek Linkens, and owe gratitude for relevant information to Donald Hinchcliffe and to my late dear friend and advisor, Peter Fenwick.

In my concluding years of life the opportunity to work with Chinese students has enriched my days. This could not have been without the help of Dorothy, along with Robert and Barbara Storrey, and Ruth Cockram, for their welcome part in entertaining students.

Our lives do not all fall into one pattern. It has been given to me to see the centenary year of my birth, but I commend to every reader the words of Richard Baxter's hymn,

> Lord, it belongs not to my care
>   Whether I die or live:
> To love and serve Thee is my share,
>   And this Thy grace must give.

DOUGLAS HIGGINS
Gleadless, Sheffield
May 2014

I

Light in a South Yorkshire Village

I was born on the 16th of August 1914, a few days after World War I began, the third child of Arnold and Annie Higgins. My older brother and sister, Cecil and Winnie, are twins, and I was followed by Leslie and Marjorie. My father and mother had come to live in Gleadless, a small village in the West Riding of Yorkshire, about 1912. Although only five miles from Sheffield, it was accessible only by a roundabout route, which made it remote at that time. My earliest memory is of my mother closing the shutters because a German Zeppelin was over Sheffield. That was in 1917. An early memory I have of my father concerned an event on the 15th of July, 1923. It was a Thursday afternoon, the day my father had an afternoon off, and on returning from school I found him working hard in the garden. Our attention was on the sky which was a forbidding colour of dark copper, and the forerunner of the greatest storm we ever knew in Sheffield. There was little sleep that night and few children in school the next morning. The newspaper headline the next day was, 'Sheffield's Night of Terror'.

At that point I was still in Gleadless Council School, which I had entered when nearly five years of age. My father had high hopes for us, and at his request, along with my older sister and two brothers, I was transferred to Manor Council School on City Road in Sheffield about the age of ten. This meant for us a walk of one mile from our village to Manor Top, where we could finish the journey on a tram for the price of a halfpenny. After Gleadless was included within the city boundary in 1921, the route to school was made more direct by the construction of Ridgeway Road in 1922–23. I attended the Manor School for little more than a year when, on passing the so-called eleven-plus exams, I was awarded a scholarship to Central Secondary, a grammar school in Orchard Lane, Sheffield.

There I remained for four years until I was sixteen in 1930. I took particular interest in history and English literature, but I came to realize that I had a more than average ability for drawing. This was confirmed, to my surprise, when in my third year I was awarded the school prize for art, and the success fuelled a consuming desire to attend the Sheffield School of Art. So when I left the grammar school the next year, without qualifications or regrets, I was satisfied to have won a scholarship for evening classes at the Art School. The building in Arundel Street presented a unique Byzantine style frontage, which, unfortunately, was destroyed in the blitz of 1940. It was the training ground for a number of eminent artists.

Douglas (second left) with his older sister Wynne (to the left), brothers Leslie and Cecil, and younger sister, Marjorie

My father was a chemist's assistant and worked in several branches of Boots, the pharmacy, one in Attercliffe and another in Heeley Bridge. This frequently meant lengthy walks for him, but we all grew up to consider walking as no hardship. As children we would often go to meet him coming home from work. On one occasion my father and I walked to Worksop, a distance of 18 miles. After a short time we welcomed the arrival of second-hand bicycles into the family. I must have been 21 before I had a new one of my own—a Raleigh. With this there were to be lengthy summer rides. On one occasion with a friend, Albert Smith, I cycled to Liverpool in one day. Another much longer outing took me and another friend, Ted Fry, down to Looe in Cornwall, where we then turned east, right along the south coast and up the east coast as far as Lincolnshire, before heading for home.

Gleadless was a village in which we knew everyone. There was no doctor near at hand, and there were not the same rules on the administration of medicines as exist today. This meant that our home was also something like a pharmacy, with a cupboard full of medicines for many ailments.

The 1930s were the years of the Great Depression, and money and jobs were scarce. I had to look for daytime work and my first job was as an assistant to a Commercial Artist, who drove about the country in a large Wolseley car, and whose assistants called on shops and businesses. We travelled as far as Dumfriesshire in southwest Scotland. At that time I had no experience of the world, and it was my mother who first recognized that my employer was not only a heavy drinker but a thoroughly immoral man. My work with him was speedily ended! Later I found settled employment with

Thomas E. Atkin who owned a reputable firm for commercial art-work in Sheffield, where my main role was the design of displays for shops and cinemas.

Throughout the 1930s I continued to attend evening classes at the School of Art. That period was a new chapter in my life, in part due to the relationships formed with a number of other people. One of my contemporaries was Lewis Lupton, whose father was the pastor of a Strict Baptist chapel in Sheffield, but Lewis was not a Christian then, and we did not get to know each other. Two fellow students, whom I have already mentioned, Albert Smith and Ted Fry, were to become life-long friends. Besides cycling, we shared an interest in elementary astronomy and space travel, which at that time, was just science fiction. This mutual interest was increased when we were invited to visit the small observatory in Weston Park, and were fascinated with the view of the heavens through the six and a half inch telescope. At the observatory we met a professor who taught at the university. He invited us to attend his astronomy class, which we readily accepted.

To me, at that time, the university was a venerable institution frequented only by the well-to-do and the super-intelligent. I now realised that the four years I endured at the grammar school had not been entirely fruitless. A latent desire for more knowledge had been created by one or two subjects, and now it was increased when I became aware of the learning and facilities available at the university. So I enrolled in a physics class.

I was now about eighteen and was having serious thoughts about the fact that *I could not live as I ought*. These thoughts grew more intense, and were exacerbated by my inability to relate what I had absorbed without question as a school boy to what I was now learning in science about the universe.

I was nurtured in a Christian environment. The Bible, made familiar in Sunday school, and at church services at the local Congregational church, though little understood, had established its authority, coloured my thinking, and moulded my lifestyle. Gently but effectually it had enlightened my conscience and heightened my self-awareness. Consequently, I was often occupied in trying to accommodate my established ideas with the information received in university lectures. My fragile complacency was now being disturbed by serious doubts about the existence of God and the truth of the Bible. But even more disturbing was the unwelcome intrusion into my mind of ugly thoughts and evil desires, which, I fondly imagined, I could remedy. Surely, I thought, more diligence, greater devotion and practical involvement in religious duties was the answer. But it wasn't.

Dismayed, because the situation seemed to worsen, I turned to the Bible, and read the parable of the good Samaritan. But what a disappointment! Jesus, I thought, was evasive, for instead of telling the man clearly what he must do, he told him a story of a man robbed and injured on his journey from Jerusalem to Jericho. That, to me in my ignorance, was no answer.

At that time, when I yearned for a real knowledge of God, a Christian preacher used to be a regular visitor to our home. Putting on a brave face to hide my rising concern, and assuming a casual interest, I questioned him hoping to receive a rational explanation of the problems which were distressing me. Why Christ had to die for my sins I could not understand; and when one is uncertain of the existence of God, to be told that the justice of God demanded it, is simply to add yet another uncertainty.

Though in a state of some discouragement, I continued my regular attendance at the services of the local Congregational church. By this point I had been elected to teach in the Sunday school. Regrettably, it was a case of the blind leading the blind both in the church and the Sunday school. I received no help whatever from the preaching, and was inclined to think that Christianity was simply a matter of opinion. Of course, part of the problem lay with me and not with what I heard or read.

While I feared my former ideas and opinions were inadequate, I was reluctant to let go of them. Groping around in this twilight state of mind I could not but compare it to the light that appeared to pervade my university studies. The latter were so logical. Their conclusions so certain, like the theorems of Pythagoras, I had committed to memory in the geometry class at the grammar school.

I was now spending three nights a week at the university and two at the Art School. But as my studies progressed I became more convinced that the universe was the work of a Creator; but where was the proof? Was he the God of the Bible, and could he be known? Overshadowed with these questions, I continued my lifeless worship of an unknown God, but things were soon to change. Unknown to me, I was being led by an unseen hand.

Along with other members of a Christian Endeavour meeting, I attended a service with members of a similar group in a church a few miles away. The time we shared was pleasant and profitable. I remember nothing of the first such meeting except the words of the closing hymn,

> Oh for a faith that will not shrink,
>   Though pressed by many a foe;
> That will not tremble on the brink
>   Of any earthly woe.

This hymn voiced the deep yearning of my heart, experienced for so long, but it intensified rather than satisfied that yearning. I returned home disappointed and distressed, wondering what more I could do. Straight to my bedroom I went. Dropping to my knees, and lifting my hands to heaven, I said with desperate seriousness, 'If you are God in heaven, and have any love for me, then you must do something about it, or you can put my name down for hell, and I'll be there as sure as the sun rises tomorrow.'

Immediately I felt a sense of relief, such as one might physically feel after being held down and then released. I saw nothing, I heard nothing, I knew nothing, but this:

there is a God and he had made himself known to me.

But an insatiable desire to know more set me searching every available source. I understood little of the Bible, and the sermons I heard added nothing to enlighten me.

At the university I had now moved on to an evening class of lectures on biology, given by a Professor Eastman. In the course of the lectures one of his remarks set me on a new track. He recommended a book on biology by an Edinburgh professor. When I borrowed it from the university library, it seemed to me that the author was a Christian because he quoted from the Bible, and this led me to think that a scientist might give me a better foundation for religion than the Christians of my acquaintance who seemed to put forward only their own ideas.

I was now working as a display artist for Thomas Atkin, preparing advertisements and promotional material, and Saturday afternoons were the only times I had free. These I started to give to searching the science section in the Central Library in Surrey Street, looking for a book to help me. Week after week I scanned the shelves, picking out any title which looked promising and flicking through the pages. I kept no record of the number of visits I made, but a hope engendered by that bedroom experience encouraged my endeavour, and so I continued to visit the library. The year was 1936, and I had celebrated my twenty-second birthday, but I was still walking in darkness and had no light. I recall, sitting alone, reflecting on my failure, and saying to myself, I must make one last attempt, one more library visit. I tried to shake off a sense of desperation by attempting to divert my thoughts to other things.

Then came a Saturday afternoon not to be forgotten. I was at the library as usual, continuing my now familiar round of inspection, reading the titles on the spines of books, and occasionally taking one from the shelf to read more. On this particular day my eyes fell on a volume with the title, *Natural Law in the Spiritual World*, by Professor Henry Drummond, who I understood to be a zoologist. I paused for a moment and said to myself, 'Law and order—that's what I need for my chaotic thinking.' On opening it, I found some technical language which would have put me off had it not been for the biology classes I had taken. The first chapter addressed the law of biogenesis but I knew what that was all about.

I left the Central Library clutching Drummond's book as if it had been a wad of banknotes. The author was a scientist and a Christian and it seemed to be the very book I needed. Arriving home, I sat down beside the open fire, determined to read every word. I did not need to do so, for I was only a few pages into the first chapter when I read these words, quoted from the New Testament,

> He that hath the Son hath life, and he that hath not the Son hath not life (John 5:12).

Stunned, I realized what was the obvious truth: to know Jesus Christ is to have eternal life! I said almost audibly, 'You fool, to think that you can give yourself life; only Jesus can give you life!' My world turned over. The experience was like being blindfolded, taken to an unknown place and then having the blindfold stripped away. The ecstatic joy I felt cannot be described, but it must have been apparent in my whole appearance, for my younger brother, entering the room at that moment, said derisively, 'You're going round the bend, you are!' Ignoring his remark, I raced upstairs to my bedroom and, again falling on my knees, I said out loud, 'Now I know you, blessed Jesus!'

On several occasions, that same night, I awoke conscious of the presence of Christ. I came to know what the Puritans meant when they spoke about 'bounty money', for I experienced the Holy Spirit's power in subduing the power of sin, so much so, that I erroneously concluded that the battle was over. Though I doubted his words at the time, the warning of an elderly Christian proved to be true: the battle had just begun.

So this was why I was led into the biology class. How true it is,

> God moves in a mysterious way
> His wonders to perform.

A few years later I penned these lines to give expression to the sure and certain hope that I had found in Jesus Christ:

> When I the word of God peruse,
> And see the Name of Jesus used;

> I marvel that that Name can be
> Just printed like the rest I see;
> For now I know that Name contains
> A power above all other names.
> My hope, my Saviour, Husband, He,
> 'Tis God's great Name, who died for me.

While I was secretly rejoicing, I felt a sense of loneliness. Something had happened to me that I supposed had never happened to anyone else. If I told people that I loved Jesus, they would think me effeminate. But I had to tell someone, so I decided to tell the minister of our local church. He would understand, I felt sure. At the conclusion of an afternoon service, I waited until the congregation had left. I approached the minister as he stood at the door of the church and with some trepidation said, almost apologetically, 'I've been born again.' I couldn't help but notice how the expression of his face changed. At first he looked surprised, then puzzled, and finally embarrassed. Then with a patronizing smile he patted me on the shoulder and said, 'Very nice sonny; very nice.' I walked out of that chapel saying to myself, 'It's true something strange has happened to you. Maybe you'll be in a mad house in a fortnight.' Yet at the same time I was inwardly rejoicing.

At this time I was the assistant secretary of the Sunday School but, a few months earlier the church had asked for someone to help lead the Bible Class for young people. I volunteered and was accepted. As mentioned above, I was already a Sunday School teacher, although what I taught the children I don't know—the Lord forgive me. But now in my enlightened state, things were about to change.

Mr S., who was in charge of the Bible class, introduced me to my new duties. I was to lead the meeting one week, announcing the hymns of his choice while he would give the address. The following week the roles would be reversed; he would lead and I would give the address. I recall the first occasion when I had to speak and the joy and boldness with which I took the words of Jesus, 'You must be born again.'

I noticed that day that some of the girls looked surprised and stopped fiddling with their belongings. One girl, or should I say, young lady, by the name of Eileen Rushby, paid very close attention. She was a newcomer to the church whom I did not know. Rather shy and reserved in temperament, she did not look very pleased with what I said, but made no comment.

The reaction of Mr S. to my address I did not discover until a few weeks later when it was his turn to teach the lesson. I entered the vestry to ask for the hymn he had chosen for me to announce, but without looking at me, he said in a voice charged with emotion, 'I will have "Whosoever will…"'

During the service I prefaced the announcement of the hymn by quoting the words of Jesus, 'He who has ears to hear let him hear', and then gave out the first line, 'Whosoever heareth, shout, shout the sound.' When the service was over and the young people had left, I was berated by the very irate speaker. 'You've got to resign; I'm not having you helping me and preaching what you have been preaching', he said in a voice quivering with suppressed anger. Greatly surprised, but unperturbed, I replied, 'But why should I resign? If I have said anything contrary to the Scriptures, then I'll resign.' But he insisted, 'You've got to resign!' Upon my refusal he reported the matter to the Sunday school superintendents and I was relieved of my duties.

Thinking it over, I could only conclude that grace alone was a doctrine Mr S. disliked intensely. He must have gathered it from something I said, for at the time I had never heard the phrase 'the doctrines of grace', and knew nothing at all about Calvin and Calvinism.

* * *

Whenever the weather was favourable, a group of young people would go for a walk after the evening service. During our walks the conversation often included discussion and questions about God, the Bible, and the world around us.

One such walk ended as it was getting dark, and Eileen, the young lady mentioned earlier as being so attentive in the Bible class, and I were the last to disperse. Hesitating for a moment before turning away she asked me a question about the planet Jupiter, at that time so bright. 'I don't know', I replied, 'but one day I shall.' 'Yes', she snapped, 'I had that hope until you said what you have said'; and she was gone. What I did not know was that she had told her mother she thought me a right upstart and the only one going to heaven.

Stung by her remark that Sunday evening, I had gone but a few yards when the thought suddenly struck me, was God dealing with Eileen? Was she under conviction of sin? It turned out that she was, and that very Sunday night in a dream she felt she was sinking and called upon the Lord to save her. And he did! But I was not to know it until the following Wednesday, for though we were both present at some secular meeting on the Monday night, my innocuous but foolish behaviour deterred her from approaching me.

On Wednesday afternoon of that week, in the studio where I was working on Howard Street, I was surprised by a feral pigeon which flew in through the window and wandered about. It reminded me of the descent of the Holy Spirit as a dove at the baptism of Jesus. 'Omnipotence has servants everywhere.' Had the Holy Spirit come upon Eileen? Eager to know the answer to that question, I arrived before anyone else at the Christian Endeavour meeting which was held in the Sunday school building. The entrance from the chapel yard was through a large outer door into a porch, and then through a smaller door into the main building. I waited expectantly for a few minutes then walked to the entrance. As I opened the inner door Eileen entered the porch, so I retreated a few yards into the main building. She came across to me and, taking me by the hand, said in her modest, kind way, 'Isn't it lovely to be able to say, "*Our* Father"!' 'What do you mean?', I stammered, though I knew very well what she meant. She then went on to say, 'I now know what you have been talking about', and she went on to relate what had happened on Sunday night, and the reasons why she couldn't tell me on the Monday.

This drew me to her because I did not then know anyone else who felt the same. But we little knew that from that beginning our whole lives were to be together.

2

Early Christian Experiences

I had known the Lord about two or three weeks when, one Sunday evening, a friend and I were returning from a Christian Union service in the university. Passing by the City Hall we encountered a large group of men apparently listening to, and replying to, a speaker (a usual thing in those days).

I realised someone was preaching the gospel and replying to the criticisms then men were making against it. Being short in stature but keenly interested, I wormed my way to the front. A young man, his bicycle leaning against the wall, was being questioned by the apparent leader of the group, an agnostic, but a man with some knowledge and interest in the Scriptures. On two or three occasions when the young man hesitated in replying to some charge levied against the truth, I suggested a relevant Scripture quotation.

Eventually, the meeting closed when the young itinerant preacher said he must go, because he had to be in the hostel where he was staying by 9 p.m. As he mounted his bicycle he pointed to me and said to the leader, 'This young man will answer any further questions.'

As the crowd began to disperse, the spokesman turned and with Goliath-like contempt for the stripling standing before him flung a question at me which he hoped would lay me low. But I gave him an answer that obliged him to raise another objection. The crowd began to regroup and closed in eager to see the result of the debate. There was now no way of escape for me. I found myself completely surrounded by men whose company I would normally have avoided.

As I explained why and how I came to believe, my opponent's attitude changed and he became keenly interested. 'How could I be so sure', he insisted, 'that there was a God and that the Bible is true? Prove it!' he said.

I replied, 'I cannot, and there is only one person who can and that person is God himself. I say this kindly, but you don't believe because you *can't* believe. We are all dead in sin, as the Bible says, until God makes us alive.'

He said, 'I'm not dead!'

Alluding to a dog that was wandering around, I said, 'Do you think that dog is interested in our conversation? It's alive, isn't it?'

He didn't scorn the question like some others, but said, 'Well, it hasn't got the mental capability.' I replied, 'We can say, then, that it is dead to our dimension of life?'

Our conversation was suddenly interrupted by a surge in the crowd. It parted and an irate fellow peered into my face and in a raucous voice charged with emotion said, 'Ah, young man I once believed like you, but come back in a year's time and you'll have forgotten it all.'

The behaviour of the crowd surprised me, for with almost one voice they dismissed him with the words, 'Clear off! They're not all like thee.'

It must have been nearly 10 p.m. when I said, 'I must go.' The crowd dispersed but the leader, walking beside me, asked where I lived and could he accompany me to the bus station. And then he said, in the hearing of some friends, 'Young man, I've never heard the Scriptures defended like that. Will you come again next Sunday night?'

I am ashamed to say it, but I was afraid to meet that crowd again, so I never went back, even though I had experienced God's enabling power.

* * *

It was while attending the astronomy class as a very young Christian that I suffered an experience which dispelled any doubts I had about spirit possession. Also attending the class was a very dignified lady of a commanding presence. I don't remember speaking to her personally, but I think she must have overheard my conversation with other members. By chance I met her one day in town when she said, 'Mr Higgins, I've had an experience like yours which I would like you to hear. I also understand that you have an astronomical telescope. Please may I borrow it for a short time?' After expressing my pleasure at what she said, she gave me her address and we parted. I knew the area where she lived quite well, a small farm remotely situated about six miles from my home. With difficulty I managed to carry the telescope on my bicycle and delivered it a day or two later. There was no invitation to enter and, after her brief expression of thanks, I returned home.

How long she kept the telescope I cannot recall, but what I do remember is the strange reception I received when I returned to collect it some time later. Upon my knocking, the door opened, and from within, I heard the name Kathy. A teenage girl appeared, handed me the telescope, and said that it was not convenient for the lady to see me, and so I left. Thinking it strange, but realising that inconveniences do occur, I brushed it aside.

When, however, I paid another visit and received the same treatment my curiosity was aroused. Undeterred by these refusals—I must have been motivated by her request as well as a desire to hear her story—I made another visit.

This time I met and heard no one but Mrs W. herself, who led me into a room which we entered together. Closing the door behind her, and pointing to an armchair, I sat down. I thought how unusually silent it was for a farm.

Seated in a chair almost opposite me, she began by saying she was born in Darnall, a district of Sheffield. Brought up as a Roman Catholic she was a highly sensitive child, often emotionally disturbed by her dreams.

'Speaking as one not alone', she said, 'we eventually left the Roman Catholic Church and turned to reading the Bible. After reading through the Acts of the Apostles we then put the Bible aside.' That decision aroused both my doubts and my fears, for I knew that a genuine Christian experience is centred in Christ, of whom no mention had been made. My suspicions were confirmed when she told me that in a vision she had met and communed with a being called the 'Resurrection'. But there was more to come.

'My heavenly father', she said, 'has employed me on several errands of mercy', one of which I will relate. She was told to go to London where on Westminster Bridge she would meet a woman who intended to drown herself in the River Thames. She was to speak to her and persuade her to return home to Lancaster, which she did. But she added that she was informed a few days later that the woman had committed suicide by putting her head in the gas oven.

I might well have doubted her story but it was so well authenticated by letters and newspaper cuttings that I could not. I felt spiritually overwhelmed by what she was telling me. Then I remembered the words of 1 John 4:1, 'Believe not every spirit, but try the spirits whether they are of God.' I was gripped with the fear of attributing the work of the Holy Spirit to an evil agent. But the crisis was still to come.

Her conversation turned to events in the history of the early Christian church, of which, at that time, I knew very little. Amongst other things she asserted that the creeds formulated by the church councils, particularly that of Nicaea, were not true.

Whether it was apparent to her I shall never know, but although I was almost trembling with fear and nervous excitement, I remained silent, which she might have mistaken for submission. Perhaps this encouraged her to say more, for after a moment or two of silence she said hesitatingly, 'I would like to tell you something.'

'Well why don't you?', I said.

'I must ask my father', she replied.

Lolling back in the chair she closed her eyes and began:

'There never was a man called Jesus Christ, it was a myth invented by the Papacy.'

That lit the fuse, but to be sure I had heard aright, I asked, 'Will you please repeat that', which she did.

Poised like a tiger about to spring, I asked the same question a second time, but before she finished the sentence I said, 'Liar!'

Opening her eyes and sitting bolt upright she said, 'How dare you interrupt when I'm speaking to my father?'

'Your father is the devil', I replied.

'There isn't a devil!', she snapped.

Grasping my Bible, and reminding her of the sovereignty of God, I left the house and this angry woman. It was midnight and dark. Afraid, I jumped on my bicycle and I must have broken the cycling speed record, only to find when I arrived home that I left my scarf behind. I vowed never to tempt Providence in retrieving it!

* * *

I had known the Lord only a few months when the following incident made me realise that conscience is no infallible guide in Christian behaviour unless it is informed and regulated by the Holy Spirit and Scripture truth.

In my work as a commercial artist I was given the job of producing a display board for a large firm that sold furniture. I finished painting the background design, and was about to write the slogan, which read, 'THE GREATEST THING IN THE WORLD IS A HOME FURNISHED AT CASTLES.' That's not true, I thought. The greatest thing in the world is to know Jesus Christ. 'You can't write that', said the tempter: 'You know what it says in Hebrews 10:26, "If we sin wilfully after we have received the knowledge of the truth there remains no more sacrifice for sins."'

I tried to brush it aside, 'It's only an advert', I said to myself. But the tempter's fiery dart had hit the target. It was near closing time, so I spent the remaining minutes needlessly touching up the background of my design, and hoping the journey home would dispel my rising fear. But it didn't. The wound was too deep. It disturbed my sleep, and I rose in the morning determined to tell the boss that I couldn't write the slogan. If he sacked me that would be a serious matter, for there were very few commercial art jobs in Sheffield in the 1930s. When

I arrived at work I was feeling strangely confused and on the verge of tears. Nevertheless, I found the boss and said, 'Mr Atkin, I can't write this.'

Mistaking my word *can't* for incompetence, he said, 'Of course you *can*. You've written dozens.'

I said, 'I mean, can't do it *conscientiously*; because it's not true; the greatest thing in the world is to know Jesus Christ.'

'Well, I'll do it', he said, almost sympathetically.

Like a man relieved of a crushing burden, I lifted my heart to the Lord in gushing gratitude.

* * *

During this time the trouble which had arisen through my assisting Mr S. with the young peoples' Bible Class had not gone away. My protest at being asked to resign had been brought before the church officers, who requested that the minister deal with the problem, and show me where I was wrong. I cannot recall that he ever interviewed me privately, but he did make several oblique attempts to put me right in his sermons.

Since nothing had been settled, an appeal was made to the ministers of three Congregational churches in the city. Two of them, it was said, refused to be involved in such matters, and declined the invitation. Only one was willing to come and a date was duly arranged. In addition to the church officers and Sunday School teachers who were to meet him and me, four other friends from the class wanted to be present, including Eileen who was no longer a mere spectator of spiritual things. So I didn't stand alone the day the minister breezed into the room, saying how pleased he was to meet young people with opinions of their own. I am inclined to think he probably regretted his opening words later. Apparently someone must have told him that I was the trouble maker, for he immediately began to question me, never once appealing to the others.

I now remember little of what he said, but I sought to answer every question by referring to the Scriptures, while he made no such reference. As his interrogation continued I noticed that my biblical replies were making him more and more irate. Eventually his patience snapped. He leaned forward over the table at which he was sitting, looked at me intently, and said: 'You're a psychological case, you are!'

To this I replied, 'If they have called the Prince of the house Beelzebub, how much more will they call his servants?'

What followed surprised everyone, for he dropped his gaze, picked up his brief case, and without a word of by-your-leave, he hurried out of the building and was gone.

The embarrassing silence that followed was broken by a critical remark about his whole conduct. The appeal by the church officers for outside help had proved that the problem was not simply about my resignation. It was about biblical truth. The minister had failed to expose my teaching as heretical, and the question of what was to be believed remained. However, certain individuals were still determined to get rid of me. Consequently, I was summoned before the whole congregation to be told by the church secretary that I must be removed from the office of Sunday school assistant secretary, and from any other position which I held in the church. They were obliged to do so, he said, because I was preaching contrary to the confession of faith adopted by the church when it was founded in 1829. But there was no copy of the confession available to substantiate his claim. The document, I was told, had been deposited with a church in Bradford years ago. It was after a later congregational meeting that an old lady approached me and said, quite innocently, 'Would you like to see a copy of the confession?' 'I certainly would', I replied.

A few days later she lent it to me, and I read it. To my surprise, the articles of faith were prefaced by what was virtually a warning which required the removal from office of any minister who failed to subscribe to the articles generally known as the doctrines of grace.

Preserved by God's grace from fostering any bitter feelings toward anyone, I decided to reveal the truth regarding the church's confession. It would mean exposing the fallacy and wrong in the church secretary's pronouncement. My keenest opponents had concluded that the matter was settled. I was not to be allowed to preach or teach in the church, or on church premises.

One day I was talking to an old man outside the church. He was a stone grinder and was very deaf. As we conversed out on the street, the minister's wife came up and stood right between us with her back to me: 'Don't listen to a word from him', she said to the old man. She then turned and walked into the church. The old man looked at me and, cupping his hands behind his ears, asked, 'What did she say?' I replied, 'Oh, never mind!'

However, that bitter attitude was characteristic of only a few of the church folk. My relationship with the secretary was cordial. He had known me from childhood, and I respected him. It was with no malicious intent, therefore, that I decided to expose the fallacy and reveal the truth of the church's theological position.

The news had spread, the school room was full. The minister opened the meeting, making only a brief reference to the business in hand.

Once again, and it seemed to me, almost apologetically, the secretary repeated the charge against me, which the opposition confidently thought would end my activities in the church. I stood up, faced the congregation, and said, 'You will notice that Mr G. has not produced a copy of the confession which I have read. If he did, then he might not be in charge of this church.'

The leader of the Bible class, who demanded my resignation, jumped to his feet and shouted, 'Cross his name off the books!', which was ultimately done, even though, when a vote was taken, the opponents lost by one.

While I cannot speak for the other friends involved, Eileen, unlike me, had been distressed by the experience. The situation for her had been aggravated by a church member who, posing as a knowledgeable friend, secretly visited her parents to warn them about me and my 'erroneous teaching'.

Nevertheless, I was blessed, for I had experienced a fulfilment of the promise which Jesus made, when he said we were to take no thought as to how we should answer, when questioned by authorities, for the Holy Spirit would take control.

I didn't relish the separation from the Congregational church, for I had friends there whom I had known all my life. They bore me no ill-will. But I couldn't continue to worship there. News spreads quickly in a village, and I had reason to believe I would not be welcome in the Methodist community either.

The question was, where could I go? I continued for a short time, cold-shouldered by several persons, but happy to meet with my friends. I was particularly concerned about Eileen, whose difficulties at home continued, the result of a loving mother's unfounded fears.

The Christian visitor to my home, mentioned earlier, now gave me further helpful advice on my church situation. He said: 'You will hear the gospel faithfully preached by a group of Christians meeting in a room over Saxone shoe shop in High Street, opposite the Telegraph building. The group is known as the Sovereign Grace Mission, and the services are conducted by a Mr H. M. Platts. The entrance is up a narrow staircase, and the evening service begins at 6.30 p.m.'

When the next Sunday came, not waiting for the evening, along I went in the morning, found the place, and was warmly received by Mr Platts and his congregation. They numbered about twenty, half of them being members of the Platts family. I rejoiced to hear the truth preached, and Mr Platts was interested to hear my story. I came away with the loan of a volume of the writings of the English reformer and martyr, John Bradford, in which I read a chapter on God's election. It was a welcome confirmation of my experience.[1]

Eileen accompanied me on the morning of my third Sunday at the Sovereign Grace Mission when we were enraptured by a sermon preached on the words of the risen Jesus to his astonished disciples, 'Come and dine.' The preacher was Mr Willie Lees, once a member of the Rev. James Battersby's Anglican church, which stood at the top of Townhead Street in Sheffield. As a point of interest, it was one of only two architecturally 'classical' churches in the city. It was damaged in the blitz. The other was St Paul's, demolished to make way for the 'Peace Garden'. But it is of greater interest to Christians that James Battersby was a faithful preacher of the doctrines of grace. His collected sermons are in the Central Library, Sheffield Department.

It was several weeks before Eileen was allowed to attend the Sovereign Grace Mission again. Her caring mother, a simple baptised believer, was still being harassed by two or three so-called well-wishers. She was genuinely concerned for her daughter's welfare, but

---

[1] *Writings of John Bradford* (Parker Soc., repr. Edinburgh: Banner of Truth, 1979), vol. 1, pp. 307-330.

when eventually she saw the distress her objections were causing, she lifted her restriction.

Our mutual interest in the gospel, and participation in church activities had brought us together in a growing friendship. As a boy I had spent many delightful hours in the countryside, but now, heaven above was softer blue, earth around a sweeter green to both Eileen and I. We read the Scriptures together and lifted our hearts to the Lord in thankfulness. This was the young lady who once resented my words in the Bible class. Now we were both new creatures in Christ. The love of God shed abroad in our hearts had transformed all things.

Eileen and I would marry some years later, but other events, beyond our control, were to intervene and delay that happy day. But in anticipation of our marriage I composed the following hymn to be sung at our wedding:

'Heirs together of the grace of life.'

O God, beloved, fountain of every blessing
Grant us your presence, be our honoured guest,
Hear this we pray, our heart's most dear petition,
Confirm and bless this union we request.

Your providence has brought our lives together,
Our souls were one in Christ e'er time began,
Thus we would be, for life's brief changing moment, One in our flesh and in our hearts made one.

Teach us to love for you have ever loved us,
And to forgive for you have both forgiven,

To share our joys and bear each other's burdens
Till we exchange them for the peace of heaven.

Unite our hearts, affections, faith and yearnings,
Fix them on Christ, nor ever let them move.
Help us to live forever to your glory,
Your love, your peace, your keeping grace to prove.

Whate'er we lack to seek it at your throne Lord,
Freely to give since freely we've obtained,
In pain to comfort, cherish in affliction,
Meekly accepting what your love ordains.

When at your word dissolves this earthly union,
Which is a figure of the church and Christ,
No more to live and love as wife and husband,
We'll haste to meet our Maker Husband Christ.

Eileen Rushby and Douglas Higgins in 1940

3

Five Years with 23rd Squadron, Royal Air Force

It was not long after our ties with our former church were severed, and we began attendance at the Mission in High Street, that the outbreak of World War II came in September 1939. In 1940, I was notified to report to the Royal Air Force camp at Wilmslow near Manchester, where I did the three weeks of 'square bashing', and enjoyed it. One day I was mildly threatened by the corporal instructor. He was a Scotsman, an ex-boxer, whose surprisingly effeminate gestures amused me. Looking at me on the front line of our platoon on the parade ground, he said, 'Eh, Shorty, take that smile off your face, or I shall punch it off!'

I had studied him so intently that at the end of the three weeks I drew a portrait of him. The fellows in the billet crowded round admiringly. When it was finished one of them snatched it from me saying, 'I'm going to show this to him', and off he ran. Back in a few minutes without it, he said excitedly, 'He wants to see you.'

I went along not knowing what to expect, for a corporal in a training centre was quite an authority. I knocked on the door of his private apartment and he shouted, 'Come in.' As though surprised at my appearance, he said, 'So it's you is it, Shorty? Have you done this? How much do you want for it? I've never had a photo as good as this given to me.'

That started the ball rolling in the corporals' mess, but my posting to St Athan's RAF station in South Wales left many applicants disappointed. After that came a further posting to 23rd Squadron at Ford, Sussex, from which the squadron was to move on to Bradwell Bay in Essex.[1] It was on a leave at this time that Eileen and I were engaged and we planned our wedding for late in 1942. It was not to be, for I was suddenly put on a secret posting. All letters and other communications were stopped, so Eileen knew nothing until several weeks later when she received a brief letter from Gibraltar.

I had arrived there, along with fifty members of ground crew, by aircraft carrier from Scotland. But that was not the end of our journey. We now learned that we were to be flown by a Liberator to Malta, the island in the centre of the Mediterranean, 17 miles by 8, which

[1] Information on the squadron can be found on the web, via Google. In 1938 it had become a night-fighter squadron, flying the Bristol Blenheim. Following the outbreak of war these were replaced by the Douglas Boston and later by the de Havilland Mosquito.

was a key to naval operations and the main obstruction to the free supply of support to the German army in North Africa. For that reason it had been under siege since 1940 and battered by the Luftwaffe. When it came to the day of our flight, the pilot said, 'I am taking you to Malta, and I'm glad I'm coming back. We hope not to meet a Junkers 88 on the way because we have only got two Browning guns.' On hearing that 27 of us were to be passengers in the bomb bay of the aircraft, I asked him to be sure he selected 'undercarriage down' not 'bomb doors open'!

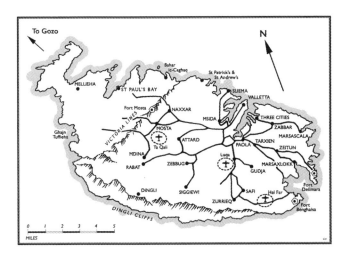

Map of Malta, 1941–42

The worst of the blitz of Malta was over by the time we arrived in December 1942 but the evidence of it was to be seen everywhere. Twenty-third Squadron was to operate from Luqa, and we, the ground crew, found ourselves housed in a former Roman Catholic building with all its windows blown out. Our beds consisted of chicken wire stretched across scaffolding, with one blanket; for meals we were introduced to pumpkin and mashed-up biscuits which had been salvaged from a sunken ship in the harbour.

As we were all accommodated in one large room, close contact was inevitable, and in the case of one man, John Begley, this proved uncomfortable. I soon became aware of his antagonism towards me. My very presence seemed to evoke his criticism and opposition; yet strangely enough, he often sought my company, and would even come to my defence if I was verbally attacked by anyone else. The situation did not improve when we were transferred as a body to another long, narrow building which I presumed had once been a stable.

We were now each given a folding, metal bed much to our surprise and comfort. I set mine up near to the end of the building and John, following close behind, chose the space immediately beside me. Thinking it might just be a temporary arrangement, using his nick-name I said to him, 'Are you going to leave your bed there, Taff?'

'Yes, Higgins, I am going to make your life hell!'

Just how he intended to do that I did not then know, but he did not keep me long in suspense. It was one evening and, having returned from work, we were all lounging about on our beds, some reading, a few others writing letters, when John, addressing me, said with an air of contempt, 'You'd have still been running around as a heathen painted blue with woad if the Pope had not sent a missionary to England.' 'That's not true', I protested, 'there was Christianity in England long before Augustine came to Canterbury. He was sent by Pope Gregory the Great in 597 A.D., landing at Pegwell Bay in Kent.'

I didn't realise it, but I had drawn a bow at a venture. Then, remembering having seen him with a small book, which I presumed was a devotional volume produced by the Roman Catholic Church, I said, 'By the way, Taff, have you got that book with you, which I've occasionally seen you reading?'

'Yes, why?', he replied. I continued, 'Is there a list of saints in it?' Fishing in his kit-bag he found it and scanning the contents muttered, 'Yes.' 'Check as correct what I have said.' He read the words '"St Augustine, sent by Pope Gregory the First (the Great) to evangelise the Saxons. Landed in Kent in 597 A.D." You see I was right', he added.

'Is St Alban who preached in England in that list?', I then asked. With assured confidence, but never suspecting a trap, he read, 'St Alban, martyred in the reign of the Emperor Diocletian in the year 302 A.D.'

There was a moment of silence suddenly broken by a loud guffaw from the gathered group. Someone shouted, 'He's shot you down in flames, Taff.'

I didn't enjoy seeing him confused as he spluttered the words, 'A priest could explain that.'

'Sorry, Taff', I said, 'No priest can alter the truth.'

He later turned his attention to ridiculing the Bible. On several occasions he would pick up my Bible, peruse it for a moment, and calling the fellows to attention would shout out, 'Listen to this: this is what Higgins reads.' He would then read some passage or verse, which he considered humorous or absurd, much to the entertainment of the group. 'Taff', I said, 'put that book down! It is a sharp sword and will cut you one of these days.' His reply was often abusive language and raucous laughter.

A de Havilland Mosquito

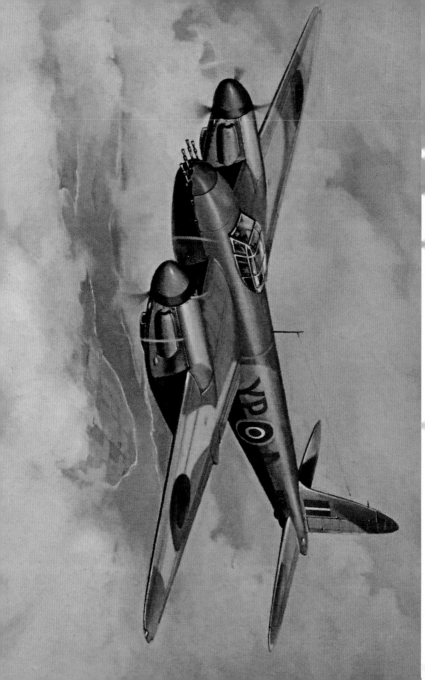

The story might have ended there and for a while it did. As the War progressed we continued to travel, first from Malta to Sardinia where, being assigned to different billets, my contacts with John were less frequent. After a short stay on that island the squadron was recalled to Little Snoring, Norfolk, in 1944 to support the D-day invasion.

By this time it had become known that I was an artist and a sign-writer. Several times whilst overseas, I had been employed in writing notices, though my trade was an airframe fitter. We had been in Norfolk only a short time when I was called to the Commanding Officer's office. He told me that the carpenter was making Honours Boards on which he wanted me to record the squadron's victories. A small inner room in a large Nissen hut was allocated for me as a work place, equipped with a long bench and adequate heating. Periodically information was given to me about the outcome of various missions.

Outside the main entrance was a concrete area on which the Navy Army Air Force Institute's (NAAFI) wagon used to stand. Personnel from the airfield came at break times for a cup of tea and a 'wad'. Among them was Taff, who would pick up his cup of tea and enter the room where I was working. On the long bench I always kept a small Bible. Invariably he would approach it, and begin turning over the pages. I noticed that when he left it was often opened at the Old Testament, generally in the prophecy of Isaiah. This practice continued for some time. Then one day he came in, and after reading for several minutes, he turned to me and in his usual arrogant tone he said, 'Well, Higgins, you don't have to be a Christian like you to know that Isaiah is talking about Jesus in this 53rd chapter.'

His words certainly got my attention, but I did not look up as I had no wish to discourage him by appearing too interested. 'Well the Jews don't believe it refers to Jesus Christ', I said, 'and I don't think the fellows in the billet would know that it did.'

Back came his reply, 'I bet you a quid they do, put your money down.'

I told him I didn't bet but he persisted, saying he would read it out in the billet that night.

I had to go to a Bible study in Fakenham that night and so was not present when he did this. On my return, quite late, I found him lying full length on my bed, his chin resting on his hand. He was reading my large Bible, which he had taken from the shelf above my bed. I gave him a nudge with my elbow and said, 'Come on Taff, off that bed, and by the way, did anybody know?' Instead of a torrent of abuse he gently murmured, 'No one knew, but just listen to these words.' In a voice charged with emotion he continued, 'These words have made me feel funny. Something has turned over inside me. I shall never again say what I have said about this book.'

I couldn't believe my ears but, gathering my scattered thoughts, I whispered, 'I told you, Taff, to leave that book alone because it would cut you one day.' Apparently he had read through Isaiah 53 and continued into chapter 54. With eyes brimming with tears he read these words: 'For the LORD has called thee as a woman forsaken and grieved in spirit, and a wife of youth when thou wast refused, saith thy God. For a small moment have I forsaken thee; but with great mercies will I gather thee.' With added emphasis he continued: 'In a little wrath I hid my face from thee for a moment; but with everlasting kindness will I have mercy on thee, saith the LORD thy Redeemer.'

What came next astounded me, for quoting the words of verse 16, 'Behold I have created the smith that bloweth the coals', he looked up and said, 'He's blowing the coals in me, isn't he?' I was shocked into silence by his interpretation. What an evidence of the Holy Spirit's power to enlighten thought! With that he slipped off my bed and without a word went to his own. I turned out the light for the others were all asleep.

It was several days later. I was again writing the victories on the Honours Boards when in came Taff with his cup of tea. Straight to the Bible he went and began reading. I occasionally gave a side-long glance but said nothing.

In a very different tone of voice and addressing me by my Christian name he said, 'Doug, I believe that there was a person called Jesus Christ as sure as I believe you're standing there, and I believe that he died for the sins of his elect people, but what I'd like to know is … was I one of them?'

I can't describe the impact his words had on my mind, and what was I to say to him? I couldn't tell him to do something, that's what Rome had been telling him all his life. 'Lord', I said, 'what shall I tell him? I will tell him you are faithful to your promises.' Turning to John I said, 'Jesus said "Come unto me all ye that are weary and heavy laden", and he didn't mean weary and burdened with hard work; he meant burdened with a sense of guilt and sin.'

The word triggered an instant reply. 'Sin', he said, 'you know something about my life but you don't know the half of it ... Jesus Christ save me?'

'Yes, John', I said, 'your sin can be as black as hell itself, but the blood of Jesus Christ cleanses us from all sin.'

He returned to his work without another word, and I fell on my knees, 'Lord', I said, 'show him Jesus, I can do no more.'

It was about 2.30 p.m. when the outer door, and then the inner door burst open and John stood before me his face like the rising sun. Without introducing the subject I said, 'Tell me, Taff, how has the Lord told you?'

Bubbling with joy he said, 'I was working on a kite in the hangar when Paddy a fellow from Southern Ireland looked up and said, 'Hey, Begley, a priest has been around wanting to know why you have not been to church.' John looked down at him from the aircraft wing and said, 'I'm not going to that church again. I'm going to read the Bible.' 'Read the Bible?' was Paddy's reply;

'You should trust in the Church and in the Virgin Mary.'

What follows clearly shows how the Holy Spirit can bring his word to mind, for John replied, '"There is one mediator between God and man, the man Christ Jesus", and "whosoever believeth in him ..."' he never finished the sentence but said to himself, 'Why am I talking like this?' The word he had intended for Paddy, the Lord turned back into his own heart. Leaving Paddy opened-mouthed, John slid off the aircraft wing and ran down to the place where I was working.

The next Saturday a former friend of John's named Jock, a Scot from Sanquhar in Dumfriesshire, told him to get ready, for they had to catch the 'liberty bus' to Norwich. It had been their practice to go drinking, usually to return the worse for drink and ready to take offence at any wrong word spoken to them. John was sitting on his bed when Jock spoke to him and, when he made no effort to get ready, Jock swore at him, emphatically reminding him that time was passing. Quietly John repeated what he had said before, 'I'm not going Jock, I've finished with that life.'

Thinking that John was just trying to embarrass me by pretending to be pious, Jock ignored it. However, when he returned from the ablutions having washed and shaved, John was still sitting there. Jock flared into a temper, swearing and abusing John, who for the third time said, 'I've told you, Jock, I've finished with that life and I'm never going again.'

I've never seen a person so nonplussed as was that

Scotsman. He couldn't utter a word. He stood for a moment like a man paralysed, then putting on his jacket he left the room. Whilst this was taking place I was silently praying. 'Hold him fast, Lord, hold him fast.'

Douglas drawing during his RAF days

John was a new creature in Christ. He never went on that bus again, but accompanied me to the Christian fellowship in Fakenham. Later he bought an old motorbike and on our Sunday day off, we travelled to Stoke Ferry to hear the Rev. Thomas Houghton, vicar of a small Anglican church. In later life, Eileen and I would visit John almost every year in Anglesey. As a trophy of sovereign grace he fought a good but lonely fight until God called him home in October 1993.

* * *

Another memory of these War years concerns our Commanding Officer in 23 Squadron, Squadron Leader Murphy. On our removal from Malta to Sardinia, already mentioned, the squadron operated from Algerho, an airfield near the coast of the north-west of the island. The nearest town of any size was Sassari, perhaps twenty miles away over wild open country, and American and British squadron vehicles were the only occasional transport. From time to time our resident personnel was joined on off-duty outings by airmen from another squadron who had served as ground staff on squadrons in North Africa. With captured German equipment, no uniform checks, and lacking a modicum of discipline, they increased a general laxity pervading the entire camp, removed as we were from the front line.

Apparently this state of affairs had become known to the authorities in Britain who dispatched a discipline unit

45

into our midst without our being made aware of what it was. I first came to know it when, working one day in the hanger, I heard someone say, 'Which is Higgins?' Having found me the fellow said, 'You're on a charge.' 'Whatever for?' I asked. 'You stayed out all night; and never booked in', was the answer I received when I reported to the Guard Room. The fact that until then we had never booked out or in, was no excuse. I was to appear before the Commanding Officer the next day.

Before I explain what happened on that occasion, I need to mention an incident that took place a few days before. My ability as an artist had continued to be used by the squadron and I was preparing a notice board record of the achievements of several aircraft which had bombed German supply trains in the Po valley in northern Italy. My work place was now the back of a room used by the CO to brief departing aircrews. On this particular occasion 'Sticky Murphy', as he was known by his peers, was speaking from a platform at the far end of the room, giving a briefing on the forthcoming night's mission.

He suddenly called out loudly, 'Higgins, write so and so', which included words I didn't approve of.

'No, Sir', I replied, 'I don't use language like that and I won't write it.'

'Go on, it's only a joke', he continued.

But I protested.

Perhaps thinking that he might be more successful, the Intelligence Officer, F. O. Lewis, who was with

Murphy, came down the centre isle and kindly but persistently tried to persuade me that it was just a joke. But it was to no avail. Having finished briefing the crew, the CO picked up his parachute and came down the aisle to the exit. He passed behind me and, without waiting for any reply, said, 'Higgins, that's a command!' I was starting to say, 'Well Sir, it's a command I can't obey', but he was gone.

The next time he saw me was when I was escorted by a sergeant to his office on the discipline charge. The CO shouted, 'Come in', and I stood, my cap removed, before his desk. Leaning back in his chair he paused for a moment, and then said, 'Higgins, I am surprised to see you here.'

'I'm surprised myself, Sir', I replied.

'Did you stay out all night?'

'No, Sir', and with a sweeping wave of his hand he said loudly, 'Case dismissed.'

Squadron Leader Murphy was a very courageous pilot. He was shot down, I heard later, over Holland. The motto of 23rd Squadron was *Semper Aggressus*, 'Having Always Attacked', and we were not lacking men who exemplified these words.

*Wycliffe Chapel, the old 'Tin Chapel' on
the last Sunday before demolition, and below
the new building (photos by John Lintern)*

4

Wycliffe Chapel, Hickmott Road

When I returned to England in 1944, Eileen and I were married on 16 August (my 30th birthday) by Mr Platts. During my absence from Sheffield the room in High Street, where we used to meet for services had been destroyed by enemy action, and our marriage service was held in Nether Chapel, where a room was now leased by the Sovereign Grace Mission. Three other friends from Gleadless Bible class days had also started to attend the meeting.

A year later, when the War ended in Europe, and I resumed civilian life, I found another change in the Sunday meeting place. The Mission had moved to a chapel in Hickmott Road, a building which had, for a short time, been occupied by the Fitzwilliam Street Open Brethren. It now came to us as their former premises, badly damaged in the blitz, had been replaced.

The Hickmott Road chapel had been built by a Mr Vince in about 1902. On Sunday, 5 June 1945 the last

Douglas and Eileen's wedding day, 16 August, 1944. Best man – George Taylor; chief bridesmaid – Enid Taylor (George's sister); younger bridesmaids – Pamela Dalton (left), and Pauline Plant (right)

service was held in Nether Chapel and on the following Wednesday the group met for a thanksgiving service in Hickmott Road. It was the week of celebration for the end of the War in Europe. Not all the young men who had left to serve their country would return. Leslie, the eldest son of Mr and Mrs Denham, was killed in North Africa in 1942.

According to a short account written by Eileen, only an evening service was held in the building at the time the War ended. It was attended by several old ladies and by one old gentleman who played an equally old pedal organ, and who appeared quite unmoved if, having begun together, the congregation finished several notes ahead of him. Now anyone who knew Mr Platts, will realise that such a situation could not last very long; nor did the organist and the congregation.

The building itself was in a very poor state. It stood on two floors, the exterior clad with corroded corrugated iron, and the interior lined with varnished boards through which the wind could pass. The congregation met on the upper floor, with a platform ascended by wooden steps as a pulpit, and a small vestry at the far end. It was heated by a huge solid fuel stove with the flue pipe going up through the roof. The lower floor, really a basement, was cold, damp and occasionally flooded, and utterly unsuitable for any church activities.

For a nick-name this building was sometimes called the 'Tin Chapel'. Its original name was the Wycliffe Memorial Mission, and from that the new name came to be Wycliffe Chapel. How long we suffered the draughts and the leaking roof I cannot now remember, but Mr Moore, the clerk of works on Sheffield Corporation, along with Tom Platts, a foreman joiner, relined and painted the whole interior, installing a new heating system. Effective treatment to stop the flooding of the basement had to wait longer.

Such was the building, but what about the living church? In my opinion the church that met here was virtually an autocracy, for whilst Mr Platts and Mr Denman, founder members, frequently preached, and a Mr Lees occasionally, there were no elected officers, no recorded members, and consequently no church meetings. Only when everyone serving in the armed forces had returned from the War, were four or five young men chosen as deacons; but, if I remember correctly, we played no active part as such. Until his death in 1955 Mr Platts held the reins.

During those ten years the usual sequence of events was occasionally interrupted by visiting preachers approved by Mr Platts. The most frequent of these was the Rev. Terence H. Brown of the Trinitarian Bible Society. But a more authoritative and influential visitor was Alfred W. Light of London, a representative of the Sovereign Grace Union (SGU), of which the church was a member. This amicable gentleman's name belied him, for he was a large man, with a full and beautiful resonating base voice that competed with the panting strains of the pedal organ. But his influence extended beyond organs.

I recall with what pleasure and profit I first heard Mr Light speak. It was in the upper room in High Street. I had known the Lord only a few months, and as yet had failed to see Christ in the Old Testament Scriptures. Mr Light's subject was the covenant God made with Abram. My doubts disappeared as he explained the significance of God's confirmation of that covenant, as recorded in Genesis 15.

Some people found his delivery distracting for when reading he pronounced the '–ed' on the past tense of every verb. He was also an able author and historian as his volume on the Nonconformist burial ground at Bunhill Fields, London, showed.

Alfred Light was one of just two persons to whom Mr Platts clearly deferred, and it was his proposal which led to the starting of a day conference in the spring and autumn. His last visit to Wycliffe Chapel was as a speaker at the April Conference in 1954. The other person whom Mr Platts obviously respected was the Rev. Basil Brunning, also from London. This exuberant gentleman was one of the speakers at the spring conference of 1952, alongside Mr Light and the gentle and scholarly Rev. Tom Shaw, vicar of North Frodingham in East Yorkshire.

I think it was on Mr Brunning's second visit in 1950 that the following amusing incident occurred. Mr Platts himself, along with a Mr T. Cornthwaite of Ribchester near Preston, were the other speakers at that spring conference. Mr Brunning was preaching and overrunning the time allotted, when Mr Platts who was sitting below the pulpit, and without turning, put his hand through the open rails intending to tap Mr B's shoe as a further reminder, for he had ignored a warning cough, that it was time for him to finish speaking. Mr Brunning, however, was determined to complete his sermon, and being fully aware of Mr Platt's practical protest, he trod on his fingers.

All these speakers had links with the SGU and the primary purpose of the conferences was to promote the doctrine of the sovereignty of the grace of God at a time when that truth was seldom heard and commonly denied. Though very strict and critical of all that was said and done, Mr Platts was a timely help and encouragement to me during those spiritually formative years. Many good and long out-of-print books he gave or lent me. The remembrance of my previous ignorance had taught me to be careful before rejecting any information contrary to my ideas and concepts.

By grace given, I was enabled to accept our pastor's corrections and rebukes, even when publicly, and unjustly on a few occasions, administered. On one occasion when Mr Platts had asked me to speak, I preached from John 12, where Jesus says, 'If a grain of wheat falls into the ground and dies, it abides alone.' When, during the sermon I said, 'I think that this word "die" needs some explanation, because it does not mean rot, but dying in one form and coming up in another', Mr Platts, who used to sit in an armchair below the pulpit, shouted out, 'Oh, no! It is *die, die, die!*'

On another occasion I was with two of the Platts' grandchildren who, knowing that I possessed an astronomical telescope, had asked if they might look through it. I chose a clear night when the moon's surface appears most interesting, and took the telescope up to their Grandpa's house where they were staying at that time. Their first and eager question on viewing the moon, was to ask, 'What are the holes in it?' 'They are craters', I replied, 'rather like volcanic craters on earth.' But I was careful to add that astronomers were not sure whether they were made by volcanoes or, like a large stone thrown into thick mud, made by large meteorites hitting the surface, for there is no atmosphere on the moon to burn them up before they land.

Mr Platts was, all this while, standing at the open door, and heard our conversation but never came to look through the telescope, or made any comment. However, on the following Sunday morning, during his sermon, he took the occasion to say that people who say that there are craters on the moon are teaching error and speaking contrary to the word of God. One wonders what his comments would have been had it been suggested that men would one day actually land and walk on its surface.

What I owe to Mr Platts makes me hesitant to say that his teaching was unbalanced, but it was, and his mistake underlines a lesson needed whenever Calvinistic belief revives. He rightly emphasized that salvation is the gift of God, but there was little or nothing heard of Christ's invitation to sinners to come to him, nor guidance to hearers on how they could become Christians. He was also inclined to teach that unless you had a sensational conversion, you had reason to question whether you were saved at all. These deficiencies had much to do with the congregation's lack of growth. From time to time newcomers would come but they seldom stayed. Eileen's sister, Ada, is a case in point. As soon as she appeared in the congregation, Mr Platts turned all attention to 'the doctrines of grace'. She would not come for ages after that, and, although a Christian, found those doctrines uncomfortable for a long time. Eventually, after Eileen and I had explained things to her, she came to know the truth more fully.

Harry Platts

I cannot give the exact figures, but at the time the church moved into Hickmott Road Chapel its congregation was probably about twenty plus. Mr Platts provided a record book which was signed by every preacher morning and evening. It also recorded their sermon texts and the hymns which were chosen. The first record was for Sunday, 11 November 1945, when the preacher was Alfred Light.

Mr Platts preached his last sermon on the morning of Sunday, 13 February 1955. Before the War and while we still worshipped in the room in High Street, I was invited to preach occasionally. But after my return in 1945, the invitations were much less frequent and it was only after the demise of Mr Platts that I shared the ministry with Mr Denman and Mr Platts' son, Jim.

Sometime in 1948 I accompanied Mr Platts to an SGU conference at Grove Chapel in London. It was there that I heard the Rev. Charles Breed, who was the Principal of a Strict Baptist college, and whose accent marked him out as a Cockney. I enjoyed his sermon immensely. To me it was an eloquent, logical and doctrinally substantial presentation of the gospel. But to Mr Platts, so proud of his Yorkshire accent, it afforded no benefit or blessing. My suggestion that he should be asked to speak at one of our conferences was casually dismissed.

The year 1954 ushered in a change which was to affect many of the churches in Sheffield. It was the first visit to Britain of the American evangelist Dr Billy Graham, whose sermons were transmitted live to relay services in many cities around the UK including Sheffield. Regrettably the congregation at Hickmott Road was discouraged from attending the meetings.

I was, however, drawn in because of the liberating blessing those services were for many. Most of the young people who were then converted, including many who attended the various churches, had never received any scriptural instruction. It was therefore decided to invite them to follow-up meetings, which were to be held each fortnight, where they would receive basic Bible teaching.

The first few meetings were in very humble and limited premises, which gave rise to the name 'Youth Squash', a name that stuck to the meeting for the next twenty-one years of its existence. The organizer was Keith Hood who had returned from America where he had studied theology and had experience of ministering to young Christians. When he moved on he appointed Peter Fenwick, a student at the university, aided by John Green, as the leader in these new meetings. To my surprise he asked me if I would solemnly promise to support Peter, particularly doctrinally, while he remained in charge. I gave him my promise, and Eileen and I were invited on to the committee a short time later. Regrettably, my involvement was frowned upon by one or two at Wycliffe Chapel, but the prejudice and unfounded fears were to melt away due to the increasing contacts and wider fellowship to which the Chapel members were introduced.

God solved the problem of limited accommodation through the kind intervention of Colonel Wardlow, who made it possible for the Youth Squash to meet in Surrey Street Methodist Church on Saturday evenings every fortnight. An electrical fire which destroyed the building several years later compelled the even larger numbers to seek and find accommodation in Scotland Street Methodist Church, from where it later moved into the Memorial Hall, which was part of the larger City Hall.

Through all of these activities I came to know and be known by Christians from other churches in Sheffield and further afield. In fulfilling my promise, I took every opportunity to help Peter in preaching and teaching the truth as it is in Jesus.

After Mr Platts had passed away, I invited the Rev. Charles Breed to speak at the spring conference at Wycliffe Chapel on 5 April 1956. With Peter's consent I also announced the meeting at the Youth Squash. The response was remarkable. The 'Tin Chapel' in Hickmott Road was filled to capacity. One lady and her husband, whose two daughters were diligent workers in the Youth Squash, were present. Shaking hands with me as she left, and visibly moved by what she had heard, she said, 'Oh, I've never heard grace preached like that before!'

Such a feast of gospel truth as was enjoyed on that occasion, was, though unknown to us at the time, being spread every Lord's Day before the congregation in Westminster Chapel, London by Dr Martyn Lloyd-Jones. Crumbs from that table were also beginning to fall far and wide. Some of them reached us through the preaching of O. R. Johnston whom I invited to

Wycliffe. Raymond Johnston had been one of the found-ers of the Puritan Conference at Westminster Chapel in 1950. From Oxford he had come as a language teach-er to King Edward VII Grammar School in Sheffield. Other men under the influence of Dr Lloyd-Jones, who became blessings to us, included Edwin King, Herbert Carson, and Iain Murray. They would come for the Sat-urday night Youth Squash and then take the services at Wycliffe Chapel on the Sunday.

Our spring and autumn conferences became a source of spiritual enlightenment and encouragement to many Christians, young and old. The reviving influence of the ministry received, combined with that of the Youth Squash, was to disturb the sequestered life of Wycliffe Chapel for the better. Its previous isolation from other Christian communities was due to an overwhelming fear of doctrinal contamination, mixed with ignorance of what was happening elsewhere.

It was this lack of contact which had prompted Mr Denman to ask me if I knew of anyone who would come and preach at Wycliffe. Once the door was open, the church benefitted from the preaching and the fellowship of many devoted Christians.

The fear mentioned above had also limited the church's involvement in missionary outreach. Support for work overseas went solely to the Trinitarian Bible Society. Here also the Youth Squash would play a vital part in broad-ening the interests of the Chapel as we met missionaries who had come for the Saturday night meeting but who also preached at Hickmott Road on the Sunday. Peter Fenwick, along with the entire committee, had from the beginning made missionary outreach a primary concern at Youth Squash. It began with the visit in January 1956 of Mr Roderick Davies, a missionary to Brazil. He preached and spoke about his work, first at the Squash and then at Wycliffe Chapel on a Wednesday evening.

This interest in foreign missions was further nurtured by the ongoing ministry of Mr H. Liversidge, formerly of the China Inland Mission (now the Overseas Missionary Fellowship), who, along with hundreds of other missionaries, had been expelled from China by the Communists in 1949 and had returned to Sheffield.

I am sure it was the timely ministry of many gifted members of Youth Squash, beginning with Peter Fenwick, John Green, Ray Beeley and Mike Drew, which God used to bring new life into Wycliffe Chapel. Mike Drew, originally from Dorset, had been converted through Billy Graham's preaching. After marrying Joyce, a Sheffield girl, he moved to Sheffield. They attended Wycliffe Chapel, where Mike later became an elder.

Under the blessing of God, we had seen an insular and languishing church revived. It continued to grow in numbers and influence under faithful pastors in subsequent years.[1]

---

[1] Irfon Hughes (1973–84), John Waite (1985–2000), Spencer Cunnah (2001–12), and currently Edward Collier (assistant and associate, 2005–12; pastor 2012–).

Douglas and Eileen with Andrew and Dorothy

5

Teaching and Speaking

After demobilisation from the Air Force, and return to Sheffield in 1946, my future career was not clear to me. I hoped to undertake a degree in art, studying part-time at the Art College to which my scholarship still gave me entrance. But changes had taken place there since 1939, not only in the removal to a new building on account of the bombing. The new principal did not know me and turned out to be unsympathetic to my being a part-time student while making a living by other work. A long-serving member of staff pleaded my case, however, and I was able to take up evening classes in life-drawing and pottery, which I continued into the 1950s. Other work, however, was hard to come by. My former employers, Thomas E. Atkin, could not afford to take me on, and designing greetings cards at 'Greetings Card House' was one of the alternatives I was able to find. I was not long employed there before a scheme for training ex-servicemen as school teachers was brought to my attention by the Ministry of Education, and I was asked to come for an interview. This had no immediate appeal but, when two further letters came from the Ministry, Eileen advised that the Lord was directing me towards this opportunity. So I attended the interview during which I referred to the university evening classes I had attended. As a result I was given a place at Sheffield Teacher Training College.

One of the memories I have of my time at this college is the discussions which sometimes took place during our classes. Dr Raynar, who taught history, said to me one day, 'You have wanted to ask me what I believe, now will you tell us what you believe.' Since one other member of the class was a Jesuit, the discussion that followed was most interesting!

On another occasion I painted the scene of a Sheffield bus coming up to Gleadless Townend on a snowy evening just as the sun was setting. As I worked on the painting the other students were fascinated and gathered round to watch. From then on I was often approached by the other trainee teachers for advice on their art work.

The need for more school teachers at the end of the War was such that ex-servicemen had to 'go into action' in the class room after only twelve months of training. My first appointment after qualifying was at Huntsman's Gardens School, Attercliffe, in the east end of Sheffield. It was an old school, surrounded by steel works, and was where Eileen's father had been educated. I was only working in this school for a short time when an inspector from the Local Education Authority visited the school and asked to see me. 'Look Higgins', he said, 'next Monday, don't come here; there's a job come up at Wisewood Secondary School for an art specialist. There's a big art room, and I want you to go there; so you will finish here on Friday.'

Wisewood Secondary Modern School had been built in the 1930s and was the 'show' school in the city. On my first day there I realised that the headmaster was not sure his new art teacher would be up to the standard of his predecessor. I believe his doubts were soon dispelled as I was able to demonstrate the benefits of previous experience and art training. As well as drawing and painting, I added pottery to the curriculum. My experience as a commercial artist, creating displays for shops and cinemas, was also useful in the decoration of the school hall for special occasions, such as the annual May Day celebrations and the celebration of the coronation of Queen Elizabeth in 1953. A picture of the latter featured in the Sheffield newspaper.

In 1948 Eileen and I moved into our first home. We had been living at Eileen's parents' house, where our son Andrew was born in 1946. Our daughter Dorothy followed in 1950. Two years later we bought our first family car, a 1933 Morris. The 1950s were a busy time at home with many visitors—friends, visiting preachers, students, and even Eileen's Mormon relations from Utah. The latter visitors, usually here on 'mission', soon found their attempts to gain new converts in this household prove fruitless. Eventually, we heard that I had been put on the Mormon's 'Unconvertible List'!

My mechanical training in the RAF proved useful in maintaining our old Morris car. In it we travelled to Newquay, Cornwall where we enjoyed a family holiday in 1952. When a necessary part of the petrol pump failed, en route, I was able to replace it with a razor blade! When we arrived at the camp site Eileen was somewhat alarmed because our tent was in a field separated from the stormy sea, which was at high tide, by only a small fence. However, next morning, at low tide, she was relieved to see a fine sandy beach, beyond the fence, and we all enjoyed the holiday.

Scotland was to become a favourite place for family holidays, sometimes in the company of George and Hilda Taylor and their children. I recall one picnic spot in the Highlands where I enjoyed a swim in a waterfall high up the hillside, while lunch was being prepared down below. Painting was a favourite activity on holidays, the long days allowing time for creating pictures of castles, mountains, and coastal scenes. It was a joy to be able to give the finished works away to friends. In later years Eileen and I made several visits to Switzerland where we visited Christian friends. There were also visits to Italy, Spain, and Malta, and one to Israel, where I preached in the Scottish Garrison Church in Jerusalem on the text, 'He that hath seen me hath seen the Father' (*John* 14:9).

While at Wisewood School permission was granted for me to use some preparation time to give Scripture lessons to some of the classes. These captured the pupils' interest and I often used the 'question and answer' method in teaching. The question, 'How can God speak to us?' produced the following answer from one boy: 'He can put a thought in your mind.' Another question, 'What can God do that we cannot?', led to various responses; but when I quoted the Gospels and said, 'He can tell what we are thinking', one young lad promptly confessed, 'I don't think I'd like to meet Jesus!'

After teaching at Wisewood for ten years, I moved on to other appointments in Derbyshire and Sheffield. I returned to Primary Education for my last two appointments before retiring from teaching in 1978.

* * *

Memories from family and friends[1]

At whichever school Douglas taught, his pupils soon realised that as well as his interest in art he also had a great love for the natural world. Injured or orphaned birds and animals were frequently brought to the Higgins' household to be cared for. On one occasion Douglas arrived home with a small box, and as it happened to be Dorothy's 8th birthday, he handed the box to her with a grin saying it was an extra birthday present. On opening it Dorothy found a fluffy young owl looking

[1] To the end of this chapter the pages cease to be autobiographical.

back at her! This little creature was successfully reared and released in the nearby woods. The owl was just one of many such 'visitors' which Eileen had to accommodate.

Douglas had many scientific interests and would sometimes bring out his astronomical telescope, his microscope, or his working model of a steam engine for the entertainment of visitors.

Reading was a great pleasure to Douglas, and over the years he amassed a considerable library which also meant having to make bookshelves to house them!

Despite his wide range of interests the greatest input of Douglas' Christian life was his involvement with the Sheffield Youth Squash, a work with young people which went on for over twenty years and which left a spiritual legacy in the city for which many are grateful. Douglas has given some account of this work in the preceding pages, but more needs to be said.

The work had begun through the concern of two young men, Peter Fenwick and John Green, who were students at Sheffield University at the time of the Billy Graham crusade in the mid-1950s. When the crusade had finished they started follow-up meetings on Saturday evenings in the city centre. As these meetings grew the two leaders were joined by Keith Hood, a Sheffield man who had returned from theological college in America where he had also worked with the Graham organization. Hood became the leader of the work. More people were being converted, and it was decided that mid-week meetings were needed to provide Bible teaching to some who were not well instructed in their own churches. Since Hood was preparing to go to Japan as a missionary, he handed the leadership back to Peter Fenwick and after a year in Sheffield returned to the United States for further training. By this time Douglas, about ten years senior to these men, had become involved, convinced that God's hand was on this work. Before leaving for America, Hood asked Douglas to provide the work with theological support and encouragement, which the two younger men heartily welcomed. In Fenwick's own words:

> This was a timely gift from God to John and Peter. Both had struggled at university with the generally prevailing Arminian emphasis in evangelism at that time. It seemed flawed to them but they could only grope their way through what sometimes seemed like theological barbed-wire. They knew nothing about Calvinism and though avid readers, the Christian bookshops in Sheffield did not stock books which would have been helpful. Douglas and the friendship of Wycliffe Chapel, was like a breath of fresh air. They spent many long evenings in the Higgins home, talking theology, wrestling with questions, and being introduced to authors and books such as Thomas Goodwin, Zanchius, and, most notably, Calvin's *Institutes*. Douglas had built up a marvellous library of these and many other works. They were all pretty ancient editions. The marvellous Banner of Truth was still to come.

During the 1950s the preaching 'team' at the Saturday evening meetings of the Youth Squash consisted of four 'doctrines of grace men', Peter Fenwick, John Green, Douglas Higgins, and Ray Beeley. The last person illustrates how various streams of influence were converging at this time. Ray Beeley had studied at Oxford at a time when Puritan belief was gripping the lives of such undergraduates in the Christian Union as Jim Packer, Elizabeth Lloyd-Jones, and others. Sheffield was Beeley's home town, and when he returned to be head of Scripture in a large grammar school, and lay pastor of a Wesleyan Reform church, Douglas 'found' him and invited him to a Sovereign Grace meeting at the 'Tin Chapel' at which Alfred W. Light preached on John 17. The meeting left a lasting impression on the visitor. In a letter many years later, Ray Beeley wrote of Douglas as,

> a powerful influence behind the scenes at Youth Squash. Peter Fenwick told me that he learned most of his theology talking to Douglas over the garden fence [when, for seventeen years, they were neighbours]. As I think about those days, the main impression is of the wonderful way in which God was moving. The ministry of Billy Graham brought a strong evangelistic emphasis which was greatly enhanced by the quiet but persistent efforts of those who believed in the doctrines of grace. Douglas could be very dogmatic, but always in a most friendly way, when once you got used to his finger pointing at you. I wonder whether something of this is not expressed in his portrait of Calvin!

Margaret Mitchell, regularly in attendance at the Youth Squash, said of the speakers, 'They put things in our hearts that would last forever.' There was also an international influence in a way no one could have predicted. Many of the young people involved were to become missionaries. John Green and his wife, Anne, went to Tunisia; Roy and Eunice Denton to Brazil; Geoff and Pauline Williams to India; Bill and Shelia Fernough to Japan; Mick and Margaret Foster to Papua New Guinea; Brian and Eileen Andrews to Kenya; Joan Crockford to Nigeria. At one time there were twenty-five members of the Youth Squash on the mission field and many others in training. Eileen was a faithful and much-appreciated correspondent with many of these friends serving abroad.

Don Hinchcliffe, a young evangelist with the Plymouth Brethren, warrants a fuller mention. When Eileen's sister Ada, first went with Douglas and Eileen to Wycliffe Chapel, Don warned her against the church and its teaching. A former student of Moorlands Bible College, his own preaching was to change after some students from London Bible College encouraged him to go and hear Dr Martyn Lloyd-Jones at Westminster Chapel. Don was to be the first to take Douglas to hear Lloyd-Jones and their shared beliefs sealed a life-long friendship. During the 1960s one group of young people who came to faith through one of Don's tent campaigns held in Gleadless, were encouraged to go to Douglas for weekly Bible study. They formed the nucleus of a group that grew, until over twenty young people were squeezing into the Higgins' sitting room every Monday evening. The room was later enlarged to accommodate them all!

In 1961, when Don Hinchcliffe was invited to the remote Faroe Islands, half-way between the Shetlands and Iceland, he encouraged two young men, Jogan Purkhus and Eydun Elttor, to come and study in Sheffield. For two years Douglas did much to lay the foundation for their future ministries, Jogan in Iceland and Eydun in the Faroes, where he was to become Minister for Oil in the government and leader of a large Brethren Assembly at Klaksvik, a main town in the islands.

Don's vision for training young men and women led to the establishing of St Andrew's Bible College at Malton in Yorkshire, where Douglas became a popular occasional lecturer in the 1980s. Possibly 'lecturer' is not the right term for as Don told students when they asked why Douglas did not always give printed notes of his lectures: 'You will get more out of Douglas if you don't tie him down to his notes. His extempore preaching is especially blessed by the Holy Spirit. I speak from experience.' Speaking of the influence of Douglas on the students at Malton, David Henderson, a residential lecturer remarked:

> To some of our students the doctrines of grace would appear harsh and strict, but Douglas presented them with a kindness and love which won them. His teaching came over with enthusiasm. I never heard him contradict anyone, he just projected the word. He

was an expositor, not a critic. He had an amazing overview of all Scripture, and it just seemed to flow through him in an easy way. He taught the doctrines, which glorify God, in a practical way, as natural to everyday living. It made me want my doctrines enlarged and to be practical in my own life. I wanted to be like that.

This appreciation of Douglas was not only confined to the students. Betty Henderson, the College Secretary, was known to say, 'I loved to get into his lectures and hear him teach. He was as much at home speaking when sitting in the garden as he was in the classroom. He just beamed with the truth.'

In his early life Douglas had learned that prayer was the essential preparation for preaching, and it is worth recording an incident in that connection which took place while he was still in the Air Force.

When stationed in Norfolk, before the end of the War, he used to help with a group who preached the gospel in the market square at Fakenham. One of the regular speakers, Mr W., was a sergeant and an earnest Christian, but his oft-repeated emphasis on man's ability to limit God's power to save, distressed Douglas. So when Douglas was invited to preach at the church where Mr W. attended, it became his concern to say something which could help the older man; yet how to do so without causing trouble perplexed him. He resolved to make it a matter of prayer. While sitting beneath a tree on a sunny day outside his billet Douglas got an answer as he read the Scriptures at Isaiah 48:5. There God says he has declared events 'from the beginning', before they 'came to pass', so that men do not say, 'My idol has done them.' Why, he said to himself, this was the reason why God wanted it known that we are predestinated in Christ from the beginning, to silence the idol self! 'Not of yourselves, it is the gift of God' (*Eph.* 2:8). The lasting lesson was that it is prayer which leads to speaking with God-given relevance to hearers.

* * *

One person has remained in the background in these pages, which would be in perfect keeping with her temperament; but the truth is that the wife God gave to Douglas was always at the centre of his life. She was the necessary counterpart to compliment his gifts with her own. Peter Fenwick has written:

> Douglas's wife was a marvellous hostess. While others might be talking, she would be busy cutting sandwiches and preparing other things in the kitchen. Her secretarial and organisational gifts were a major asset in the Youth Squash, where she acted as secretary for the leaders, typing letters of invitation to speakers, and maintaining contacts by correspondence to an ever-widening circle of friends. In the home she was the manager, not least in financial matters for which Douglas had no aptitude at all. While always backing him in public, like every faithful Christian wife, she would occasionally offer a word of correction.

If his enthusiasm ever tended to him exaggerating a situation, Eileen's was the steadying influence.

What they meant to each other was plain for all to see. Although Eileen was six years younger than her husband she was taken home first, dying on 12 February 1998, aged 77. In reference to his great loss, Douglas' friends would hear him quote with much feeling the verse from Charlotte Elliott's hymn, 'My God and Father, while I stray':

> If Thou shouldst call me to resign
>   What most I prize, it ne'er was mine;
> I only yield Thee what was Thine:
>   Thy will be done.

Douglas (right) with his brother Cecil

6

The 'China' House in Gleadless

After the death of Eileen, my wife, I resigned as an active senior elder at Wycliffe Chapel. It was a time when I thought that any further trips abroad and my involvement in the Lord's work was at an end, but I was mistaken.

I always had a great love of trees seeing them as one of the most interesting and beautiful parts of God's creation. I was especially thrilled by what I had read of the giant Sequoia (or Wellingtonia) trees that grow to a height of 300 feet in California. One day, some months after Eileen's death, when my daughter and I were walking in the beautiful Clumber Park, I remarked that I had always wanted to see those giant trees, but now it would no longer be possible. This was all the prompting Dorothy needed, and in September that year (1998), she and I visited the USA, first staying with Irfon and Anne Hughes in Pennsylvania, then touring California in a motor-home, before ending with a visit to the Grand Canyon and Monument Valley. It was a memorable trip, and the sight of the giant Sequoia trees was even more impressive than I had anticipated.

About twenty years earlier I had been invited to preach at a small assembly of Chinese Christians which met on Sunday afternoons in St Mark's Church, near the Hallamshire Hospital in Sheffield. This contact had led Eileen and I to befriend Ming Shu, a young Chinese lady, whose husband was working in New Zealand. This friendship with Ming Shu and her husband David grew over the years, and Eileen and I kept in contact with them even when they moved to Scotland and later returned to Singapore. When news of Eileen's death reached them they were greatly distressed but unable to attend the funeral. Instead they invited me to visit them, which I was able to do the following year when I could travel in the company of a friend. I was able to combine this trip with visits to other friends in two different parts of Australia and a short stay in Hong Kong at the invitation of other Chinese friends. The whole trip lasted five weeks, and Andrew and Dorothy now refer to it as 'Father's Grand Tour'!

In the year 2000 the Chinese fellowship moved into a large Methodist church in Sheffield which had become vacant, and being much closer to my home I was able to attend their afternoon service quite frequently. On one occasion after I had preached there and the service was over, my interpreter Hoi Fei told me that her cousin Fiona, who taught English in Japan, was coming to Sheffield on a month-long refresher course. 'But I have a problem', she said. 'I had hoped to have her stay with me in my university accommodation, but I have discovered that this is not allowed. When I enquired of several landlords, I discovered that they are only willing to take tenants for a minimum of one term.' She continued, 'Fiona can't afford to stay in a hotel for the whole month, so do you know anyone who would be willing to take her in?' Immediately the verse, 'Be not forgetful to entertain strangers' (*Heb.* 13:2) came to my mind with strong conviction. 'Well', I said, 'I have two spare bedrooms; so if she wishes to stay with me, she would be very welcome.' Hoi Fei gratefully accepted the offer.

Other students attending the Chinese church must have heard of this and shortly after, Nicole, a Christian student from Malaysia, approached me to request accommodation. She had finished her course in September but needed to stay on for the graduation ceremony in November. She too came to stay.

Again, when Nicole left, a younger pharmacology student, called Lilian, from Lanzhou on China's Yellow River, spoke to me at the church. 'Mr Higgins', she said, 'I hear that you read the Bible every night. Can I come and stay at your house?' How could I refuse such a request? She moved in to the house in January 2002 and had only been with me for a few weeks when she asked if her mother could come to visit. So, her mother arrived from China in April that year and stayed for six months. She proved to be very a friendly, intelligent, and helpful lady who gladly cooked for us all. As she didn't speak English, I gave her a short lesson each morning.

My daughter, Dorothy, had been living in Oxford-shire for some years and since her mother's death had been trying to visit regularly to help me in various ways. By 2002 she was finding the travelling very tiring and in July that year she moved to a house in Dronfield, which is about fifteen minutes drive away from me. From there she was able to be more involved with my Chi-nese visitors and to help prepare a room for each new arrival. On the second visit of Lilian's mother, Dorothy, a retired teacher, continued the English lessons with her and found her a very able pupil. Lilian stayed with me until August 2003 and returned in October the follow-ing year, after completing work experience in Welwyn Garden City, Herfordshire. She graduated in July 2005 and moved to Cardiff University, where she received a Ph.D. in Optometry.

Just prior to Lilian's return, another guest arrived. I met Celia at the Chinese church. She was a qualified accountant and was taking further courses. She stayed for two years before leaving to get married in October 2006. Due to legal reasons her marriage to her Chinese husband had to be performed in a Church of England, so the wedding was held in Gleadless Parish Church and I was privileged to be asked to sign the register as a witness. The lady minister conducted the service well and afterwards was happy to meet all the Chinese friends and family at the reception held at the Chinese church.

A month after Lilian's departure the empty room was filled by Connie Wen Sun (one of the few Chinese names I found easy to pronounce!)—so once again I had two house guests. Connie was also studying accountancy, and during her stay her mother also came to visit her. I was able to provide accommodation and Dorothy once again took up English lessons with the visitor. Connie remained with me until she was married in October 2010. Because her husband Alan, although Chinese, was born in Sheffield, they had a civil ceremony at the Registry Office in the city, at which I was asked to act as her guardian to 'give her away'. Several days later they flew to Shanghai for the customary Chinese wedding with family and friends.

Both Celia and Connie continue to live just a few miles away, so I am still favoured with visits from them, and now also their beautiful children accompany them.

Amidst all these comings and goings I have been able to introduce other Christian friends to many of these Chinese visitors. In particular Robert and Barbara Storrey have helped me and entertained many of my guests, also forming lasting friendships with them.

Whilst the majority of the students speak English quite well, their written comments in my visitors' book are occasionally quite amusing. For example, one girl wrote, 'You are the kindest man I never met'!

Even greater amusement arose on the following occasion. Rosemary was a teacher in a girls' boarding school in Derbyshire. Wednesday was her day off, and I volunteered to take her to see the Peak District; but to my surprise she asked instead to be taken to Sheffield University as she hoped to take a course in journalism there. Before going to the university, however, she requested that I check the testimonial she had brought with her. This had been written in Mandarin by her professor back in China. Instead of including the sentence: 'This student spent two weeks of her holiday assisting the professor in his researches', Rosemary's translation read: 'This student spent two weeks of her holiday *assassinating* the professor in his researches'! Thankfully the error was spotted and corrected. Rosemary was accepted on the course, later graduated, and now works for the BBC in London.

It was at Wycliffe Chapel that I first met Jane, who was to become another one of my guests from January 2007 to May 2008. I had reason to think that, like many more foreign students, she considered Christianity to be just another ideology. But, having returned to Beijing, she sent me a birthday card, on which she had written, 'You sowed the seed in my hungry heart and it has blossomed.' Apparently, God blessed his word, for she was baptised later, and her conduct and conversation during a recent visit confirmed the change.

I was ninety-six years old when Rita, my guest for a few months, left to get married. By then I was beginning to think that my offering of hospitality to Chinese students might be coming to an end. I discussed the situation with my daughter and we decided that due to my limited mobility and energy I should not have any more students to stay as it would be unreasonable to involve them in my welfare. But still feeling doubtful about this, I took the situation to the Lord in urgent prayer. 'Lord God', I said, 'I have asked you to lead me in the paths of righteousness, and guide me in all my deliberations, and to generate in my heart and mind only those desires which are in accordance with your will.' It was about a fortnight later that I had occasion to go to the Chinese church where Marilyn, a former lecturer at the university, approached me and introduced Linda, a student who had come to the university for a one-year course. 'Do you know anyone with whom she can stay?' she asked. Surely this was an answer to my prayer; so I invited her to stay at my house. But there was more to come. A few days later, when I again called at the Chinese church, a young man told me that Linda had a friend, Bonnie, who had hoped to share accommodation with her. He didn't need to say anything more, and so Bonnie also came to stay.

They arrived in September 2011. Two months later my car failed its MOT test, and I decided (with encouragement from my daughter!) that the time had come to give up driving. I disposed of the car and surrendered my driving licence. This meant I was no longer able to drive myself to visit my many friends, nor could I take the students along, or show them the beautiful countryside around Sheffield. Another problem was that of shopping, as I could no longer walk far. However, Bonnie and Linda were more than happy to help with that task, along with my daughter, Dorothy.

Linda returned to China in October 2012, and since God brought her into my life, I was encouraged to hope that he would call her by his grace. Though there was no evidence of a change, Bonnie and I continue to pray for her, for as God says, 'My word shall not return unto me empty, but will accomplish what I desire' (*Isa.* 55:11).

Bonnie went back home after her graduation, but returned as a visitor for four months and has subsequently started another course at Warwick. I owe her a debt of gratitude for her unfailing kindness, timely help, and fellowship in Christ. She is soon to be married in Birmingham, and I wish her and Leo, her future husband, every happiness. May they experience the power, the peace, and the presence of our glorious God.

I have mentioned only a few of those who have stayed with me. I am especially thankful that, with the support of family and friends, I have experienced this unexpected blessing of seeing my home used for the spiritual help and encouragement of others. One of my many Chinese guests wrote to me recently to say that she had 'never dreamed' that it would be the place where

> God would show me his mercy and love. I could not tell when and how I started to know God. But I am sure that it couldn't be separated from those times

when you explained me the Scriptures, shared your testimony, and encouraged me to pursue the truth. It was something I had never experienced from anyone. All has changed my heart from a hard stone to be soft.

The sixteen years since the Lord took my wife Eileen to glory have been filled with much kindness and love by my family and friends. My son, Andrew, now retired from a career in metallurgy, is now a grandfather himself. His wife and their family live in Nottingham and attend a large church there. Andrew has always shared my interest in aircraft and still takes me to air shows and open days at my old squadron, now based in Lincolnshire. My many friends—too many to mention them all by name—have shown me great kindness and hospitality. Some call to take me to meetings or out for a meal; such support is greatly appreciated. My daughter continues to help me in many ways and we often enjoy a drive in the country together where we love to rejoice in God's creation and talk of spiritual things. In all of this I am aware of the Lord's great goodness and provision for me as I grow older and less able to manage the everyday practical tasks.

Thanks be to God that he does not deal with any of us as we deserve! I have seen many of the promises of God fulfilled in my lifetime, but this last chapter reminds me of the words of Ecclesiastes 11:1: 'Cast thy bread upon the waters: for thou shalt find it after many days.' '*Thou shalt find it*', is the promise. If not immediately, then '*after many days*', and in some cases not until the resurrection day, when it will be fully known that our 'labour is not in vain in the Lord' (*1 Cor.* 15:58).

'Not unto us, O LORD, not unto us, but unto thy name give glory, for thy mercy, and for thy truth's sake' (*Psa.* 115:1).

Blest covenant God we hail that glorious day,
When from our eyes You wipe the tears away.
When all your saints, the world despised and loathed,
With Christ, their King, in royal robes are clothed.

Behold, this is our God, shall be our song,
For His salvation we have waited long,
Thy kingdom come, our earnest prayer we make,
When Christ, not only earth, but heaven, will shake.

To Him, the Sovereign Lord, all knees shall bow;
All enemies He then shall overthrow;
Sin, pain, and death shall be destroyed at length,
And God shall be our everlasting strength.

As the Last Adam, Jesus Christ is given
Supreme authority in earth and heaven;
And the dominion, man in Adam lost,
Will be restored when Jesus reigns at last.

We do not yet see saints in full control
Of the creation, creatures great and small;
But as a crown, Christ does that glory wear,
And all His saints shall in His glory share.

The promise made to Jesus at His birth,
As David's Son, He'll take His throne on earth;

Then Israel's gathered remnant shall confess
And own Him as the LORD our Righteousness.

The covenant promise made on oath, by God,
That Abram would possess the ground he trod;
Heir of the world by faith, with Him we're made
Joint heirs with Christ and heirs of God indeed.

Then into ploughshares men their swords shall beat,
Their spears to pruning hooks, no more to fight.
Nations shall then no more engage in war;
Nought in God's holy hill, hurt or destroy.

SOME OTHER TITLES
(WITH YORKSHIRE CONNECTIONS)
FROM
THE BANNER OF TRUTH TRUST

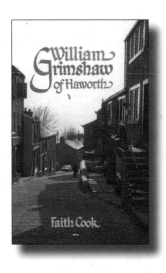

WILLIAM GRIMSHAW OF HAWORTH

Faith Cook

Faith Cook has drawn on unpublished and little-known sources to produce this comprehensive biography.

'A few such as him would make a nation tremble. He carries fire wherever he goes.' — JOHN WESLEY

'Grimshaw's unflagging energy and vigorous defense of the faith was matched by a charitable spirit that was a model of true Christlikeness . . . a surprising measure of what he said and wrote is germane to the times in which we live. This is a welcome addition to the rich treasure trove already available from the Banner of Truth. It is also a classic example of what a good biography ought to be.' — JOHN MACARTHUR

'Atmosphere, action, great character: it's *Wuthering Heights* meets Whitefield-Wesley revival.' — MIKE REEVES

ISBN 978 0 85151 734 6 (paperback)
ISBN 978 0 85151 732 2 (clothbound)
368pp.

THE LETTERS
OF
HENRY VENN

*with a Memoir
by John Venn*

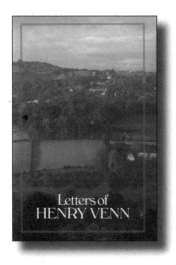

Letters of
HENRY VENN

Henry Venn (1724-1797) was the Anglican rector of Huddersfield in Yorkshire and later of Yelling in Huntingdonshire. In the twelve years of his ministry in Huddersfield (from 1759) the town was transformed from its spiritual and moral darkness, and multitudes were brought into the kingdom of God.

These letters provide a fascinating insight into the life and times of a significant 18th-century evangelical minister. They contain, on virtually every page, practical spiritual counsel of perennial wisdom applicable to a wide variety of situations.

ISBN 978 0 85151 653 0
624pp. | Clothbound

The Banner of Truth Trust originated in 1957 in London. The founders believed that much of the best literature of historic Christianity had been allowed to fall into oblivion and that, under God, its recovery could well lead not only to a strengthening of the church today, but to true revival.

Interdenominational in vision, this publishing work is now international, and our lists include a number of contemporary authors along with classics from the past. The translation of these books into many languages is encouraged.

A monthly magazine, *The Banner of Truth*, is also published. More information about this and all our publications can be found on our website or supplied by either of the offices below.

THE BANNER OF TRUTH TRUST

<table>
<tr><td>3 Murrayfield Road
Edinburgh, EH12 6EL
UK</td><td></td><td>PO Box 621, Carlisle,
Pennsylvania 17013,
USA</td></tr>
</table>

www.banneroftruth.co.uk